A FIRST *PetCare* BOOK

SO-EID-399

NITA'S
Gerbil

BY NIGEL SNELL

BARRON'S
NEW YORK

First edition for the United States and Philippines published
1989 by Barron's Educational Series, Inc.

First published 1988 by Hodder and Stoughton Children's Books,
a division of Hodder and Stoughton Ltd., Sevenoaks, Kent, England.

Text and illustrations copyright © Nigel Snell 1988.

All inquiries should be addressed to:
Barron's Educational Series, Inc.
250 Wireless Boulevard
Hauppauge, New York 11788

Library of Congress Catalog Card No. 89-257

International Standard Book No. 0–8120–6122–5

Library of Congress Cataloging-in-Publication Data

Snell, Nigel.
  Nita's gerbil / by Nigel Snell. – 1st ed.
    p. cm. – (A First pet care book)
  "First published 1988 by Hodder and Stoughton Children's Books"–
  –Verso of t.p.
    Summary: Provides information on responsible care of a gerbil, in
  such areas as bedding, cleaning, exercise, feedings, and health.
  ISBN 0-8120-6122-5
  1. Gerbils as pets–Juvenile literature. [1. Gerbils]
  I. Title. II. Series: Snell, Nigel. First pet care book.
  SF459.G4S65 1989
  636'.93233–dc19   89–257

Printed in Belgium

9012   987654321

Note to parents and teachers

These lively, colorful little books provide a splendid introduction to the joys and responsibilities of pet ownership. For the youngster who has a pet or hopes to acquire one soon, the First Pet Care series offers insights into the needs of each animal and the special friendship that can develop between it and a caring human being.

The child's need for adult supervision and support is also made abundantly clear. Thrusting too much responsibility too soon on a young person can result in misery for everyone concerned – animal, child, parent and/or teacher. While a youngster can play an important role in rearing a pet, it remains the adults' responsibility to make certain that all of the necessary care is provided. Only when this is done can the experience remain a happy and rewarding one.

Finally, it is important to stress that although many excellent and practical suggestions are made in these books, the First Pet Care series does not offer complete manuals of pet care. Additional essential information can and should be obtained from veterinarians, experienced pet owners, responsible pet dealers, and from books on the subject.

Fredric L. Frye, D.V.M., M.S.
Clinical Professor of Medicine
School of Veterinary Medicine
University of California
Davis, California

One or two?

Nita and her Dad are going to a pet store to buy a gerbil. Nita is very excited. She has helped take care of gerbils at school. But this will be the first one she has kept herself.

They talk to Mr. Jones, the pet store owner. He explains that it would be kinder to buy two gerbils. Gerbils don't like living alone.

Dad agrees, and Mr. Jones carefully packs two gerbils into a cardboard box. Nita proudly carries them home. She decides to call them Katy and Mina.

The gerbils' home

Nita's Mom helps to prepare the gerbils' new home. It is made from a fish tank with a wire cover. Inside Nita puts a mixture of clean wood shavings, chopped straw and coarse sawdust. The gerbils will dig tunnels through it and make a nesting place to sleep in.

She also puts in some hay for their bedding.

Then Nita puts a small piece of coconut shell into the tank. The gerbils will use it to play on and for chewing. Gerbils have to make sure their teeth don't grow too long or they won't be able to eat.

She also puts in some cardboard tubes for Katy and Mina to play with. Gerbils are very active and like lots of toys.

She attaches a water bottle to one side of the tank. The water bottle can be bought in the pet store. Gerbils need fresh water to drink every day.

Mom lifts the tank onto a table, out of the sunshine. The gerbils will not get too hot here.

Then Nita lets Katy and Mina into the tank. They run around, exploring their new home.

"I think they like it," says Nita. She gives Mom a big smile.

Taking care of Katy and Mina

In the wild, gerbils eat grass, roots, seeds and plants. Pet gerbils are often given special gerbil food from a pet store. They will also eat bird seed. Mr. Jones says that gerbils also like slices of apple, raw carrot and cabbage, and hay.

For a treat, Nita gives her gerbils raisins, sunflower seeds and melon seeds. Katy and Mina love them!

Leftover food should be taken out of the tank or it will rot. Be careful not to give gerbils more food than they can eat.

About every week or so, the gerbils' tank should be emptied and cleaned. Then a fresh mixture of clean wood shavings, straw and coarse sawdust should be put in. Gerbils are such clean animals that they need only a little attention to stay healthy and happy.

Nita knows that gerbils need lots of exercise. It's good for them to have a daily run outside the tank. She lifts the gerbils out one at a time. She cups her hands around them so that they can't fall.

The gerbils run around on a low table covered with an old cloth. Nita has put some toys on it. Sometimes one gerbil gets too near the edge. Nita has to guide her back toward the center. After about five minutes, Nita puts her back into the tank.

Once, one of the gerbils did fall off!
Nita couldn't see her anywhere.
But she knew gerbils love to hide. So
she looked behind the chairs and
underneath a cupboard. Then she saw
Mina peeping from behind a curtain.

Nita put a small cardboard box on the
floor, and Mina ran into it. Nita
quickly lifted her back into the tank.

Katy and Mina are both female gerbils. They play together and help to keep each other clean.

Gerbils like company. It is much kinder to keep two than just one. But they should be put together before they are ten weeks old. After that, they will fight.

Baby gerbils

If you have a male gerbil and a female gerbil, they will probably have babies. It's fun watching the babies grow, but it is often difficult to find homes for them. So it's best to make sure your gerbils are both males or both females.

You may see baby gerbils in a pet store. They stay with their parents for at least three weeks. By the age of six weeks, they should be separated into pairs.

Both male and female gerbils make good parents. They share the job of building a nest, and help to keep the babies clean and warm.

Newborn gerbils are blind and hairless. Their skin is dark red and they measure only about one inch long. But they grow quickly and are soon ready to go to their new homes. Adult gerbils normally live for about three years.

Nita takes good care of her gerbils. Her Mom and Dad help her. If one of the gerbils looks sick, they go with Nita to the vet.

Nita loves her gerbils, and hopes you like yours as much. Have fun!